# AMERICA'S NATIONAL PARKS

# AMERICA'S NATIONAL PARKS

**Thomas G Aylesworth**

**Virginia L Aylesworth**

Featuring the photos of Jeff Gnass

LONGMEADOW PRESS

A BISON BOOK

*This edition produced exclusively for Waldenbooks by*

Bison Books Corp.
17 Sherwood Place
Greenwich, CT 06830

ISBN 0–681–30380–8
Printed in Hong Kong
Reprinted 1986

*Page 1*: **The coastline of Mount
Desert Island in Acadia National
Park, Maine.** *Previous pages*: **An
autumn morning in Grand Teton
National Park. In the foreground is
the Buffalo Fork of the Snake River.**
*This Page*: **Sunrise over Crater
Lake. Wizard Island is in
foreground.**

## ACKNOWLEDGMENTS

The authors and publisher would like to thank the following people who have
helped in the preparation of this book: Richard Glassman, who designed it;
Barbara Paulding, who edited it; John K Crowley, who did the photo research.

## PICTURE CREDITS

All photos courtesy of Jeff Gnass Photography, with the following exceptions:
Alpha: 30 (top), 36–37, 45 (top), 46, 65, 75 (right), 82, 84, 88–89.
DRK Photo: 32, 34, 34–35, 38, 54–55, 56, 57.
Freelance Photographers Guild: 13 (bottom right), 22 (top), 25, 26 (left), 28
    (bottom), 33, 40–41, 48, 49, 60–61, 66, 67 (right), 70 (top), 74–75, 78
    (right).
National Park Service: 18, 51, 83

# CONTENTS

# INTRODUCTION

The awesome grandeur and majesty of America, the beautiful land, has been evolving during the millennia since the glaciers of the Ice Age advanced and retreated over most of the North American Continent. For over 100 years the most strikingly beautiful, magnificent and spectacular areas of the United States have gradually been incorporated into the National Park Service, a bureau of the United States Department of the Interior.

It all began in 1872, when the Congress established the first national park, Yellowstone, by adopting the Yellowstone Act, which set aside an area of almost untouched wilderness in Wyoming, Idaho and Montana—an area about two–thirds the size of the State of Connecticut. The Act stated that the park was 'dedicated and set apart as a public park or pleasuring-ground for the benefit and enjoyment of the people.' It also required that park regulations should 'provide for the preservation from injury or spoilation, of all timber, mineral deposits, natural curiosities, or wonders within said park, and their retention in their natural condition.'

This was an idea far ahead of its time. Much of America was then frontier land. Indeed, on 22 August 1877, just five years after the establishment of Yellowstone National Park, two tourists were killed there by Nez Percé Indians who were fleeing from vindictive US Army troops.

The Yellowstone Act became the basic guideline for the rest of America's National Parks. By the time that the National Park Service was established in 1916, 11 more parks had been added to Yellowstone. Today there are 48 of them, ranging from the unbelievably huge Wrangell–St Elias National Park in Alaska, with its 8,945,000 acres (13,977 square miles), about the size of Massachusetts and Connecticut combined, to the tiny Hot Springs National Park, with its 5824 acres (9 square miles), about 1/133 the size of Rhode Island.

These parks come in all varieties—seashore parks, estuaries and other wetlands, forests, grasslands of prairie and plains, mountains, deserts, volcanoes and glaciers. Yet all of them abide by the tenets of the old Yellowstone Act of 1872 of preservation and enjoyment.

In 1898, in praise of the United States national park system, John Muir, the celebrated naturalist, wrote: 'Thousands of nerve–shaken, overcivilized people are beginning to find out that going to the mountains is going home.' Today, the 20 million people who visit not only the mountains, but also all the other varied beauties of the national parks, understand what he was talking about. National Parks are places where young and old can exercise their minds and their bodies—many of the parks offering solitude for reflection, with a respite from the sights, the sounds, the smells and the pressures of civilization, others offering the opportunity for the thrill of discovery or the sense of wonder.

They are truly America's national treasures.

**Waterwheel Falls in the Tuolumne River Canyon in Yosemite National Park, California.**

8

# AMERICA'S NATIONAL PARKS

1. ACADIA
2. ARCHES
3. BADLANDS
4. BIG BEND
5. BISCAYNE
6. BRYCE CANYON
7. CANYONLANDS
8. CAPITOL REEF
9. CARLSBAD CAVERNS
10. CHANNEL ISLANDS
11. CRATER LAKE
12. DENALI
13. EVERGLADES
14. GATES OF THE ARCTIC
15. GLACIER
16. GLACIER BAY
17. GRAND CANYON
18. GRAND TETON
19. GREAT SMOKY MOUNTAINS
20. GUADALUPE MOUNTAINS
21. HALEAKALA
22. HAWAII VOLCANOES
23. ISLE ROYALE
24. KINGS CANYON
25. KOBUK VALLEY
26. LAKE CLARK
27. LASSEN VOLCANIC
28. MESA VERDE
29. MOUNT RAINIER
30. NORTH CASCADES
31. OLYMPIC
32. PETRIFIED FOREST
33. REDWOOD
34. ROCKY MOUNTAIN
35. SEQUOIA
36. SHENANDOAH
37. THEODORE ROOSEVELT
38. VIRGIN ISLANDS*
39. VOYAGEURS
40. WRANGELL-ST. ELIAS
41. YELLOWSTONE
42. YOSEMITE
43. ZION

✱Not Shown

Lambert Conformal Conic Projection

SCALE 1:9,000,000    1 Inch = 142 Statute Miles

©Rand McNally & Co.

9

# ACADIA

Acadia National Park is located on Mount Desert Island, Maine, about 47 miles from Bangor, and it contains the highest point of land on the US Atlantic Coast—Cadillac Mountain—at 1528 feet. Acadia also includes half of the Isle au Haut and Schoodic Point on the mainland. Samuel de Champlain, the French explorer, ran aground here in 1604, and Mount Desert Island was the scene of many contacts and conflicts between the French and the English, plus some conferences and skirmishes between them and the Indians.

Cadillac Mountain offers a spectacular view of the beautiful, rockbound coast. In the tidepools at the shore are microhabitats that change twice daily with the tides, containing almost an infinite variety of life—all exposed to view. Acadia has its forest and mountains, too, which can be explored by using its 43-mile system of carriage paths. The paths offer views of Somes Sound and Frenchman Bay, as well as beaver dams and other natural wonders. There are also some 120 miles of hiking trails in the park.

Acadia, with its 39,114 acres (61 square miles) of scenic beauty, was established as a National Park in 1919. It is unusual in that it was neither carved out of public lands nor bought with public funds, but rather was envisioned and donated through the efforts of private citizens. For example, John D Rockefeller Jr gave more than 11,000 acres (17 square miles) of land and donated the money for the carriage paths.

*Right*: **The surf along the rock–bound shores of Mount Desert Island in Acadia National Park. The rocky shoreline, hidden ledges and fog posed treacherous hazards for boats and ships until after the Civil War, when foghorns and lights were installed.**
*Below*: **Afternoon breakers on the Mount Desert Island coast. Here may be seen barnacles crowding for space on seashore rocks, rockweed, Irish moss, eider ducks, herring gulls, rock crabs, sea urchins and northern starfish.**

*Above*: Sunrise in October near Otter Point, Mount Desert Island, Acadia.

# ARCHES

Arches National Park in Utah, near Moab, contains some 88 natural stone arches, as well as pinnacles, spires, fins and windows. Once the bed of an ancient sea, the land has been laid bare by erosion, revealing the skeletal structure of the earth and turning the area into a spectacular outdoor museum. As the earth upwarped, cracks penetrated the buried sandstone layer and erosion wore away the exposed rock layers and enlarged the surface cracks, isolating narrow sandstone walls, or fins. Frost and thaws caused crumbling and flaking of the sandstone and cut through some of the fins; weathering them to form arches.

On the border of the park flows the Colorado River, where users of the Old Spanish Trail swam their mules across in the 1830s. John Wesley Wolfe, a disabled Civil War veteran, and his son Fred settled here in 1888, managing a living with their small cattle spread for more than 20 years. Arches was made a national monument in 1929 and was designated a national park in 1971.

The park, with its 73,379 acres (115 square miles) is really a wildlife sanctuary, but most of the animals there are nocturnal. It is possible, however, to see mule deer, kit foxes, jackrabbits and cottontails, kangaroo rats and other rodents, small reptiles, blue piñon jays, mountain bluebirds, golden eagles and redtailed hawks.

*Above left*: **The 'Delicate Arch' in Arches National Park. Located near the old log cabin of the Wolfe Ranch, this arch is near the far eastern border of the park.**

*Left*: **A view of the 'Courthouse Towers' and the Entrada Boulders, looking down Park Avenue in Arches National Park. Park Avenue resembles a city skyline with its balanced rocks, spires and fins.**

*Overleaf*: **The 'Landscape Arch' at sunrise in Arches National Park. It is located in the Devils Garden area in the northern section of the park.**

*Below*: **The Double Arch in The Windows Section, where four large arches can be seen from the roadway—Double and Turret Arches and North and South Windows.**

# BADLANDS

Badlands National Park is located in South Dakota, southeast of Rapid City, and appears as a fantasy of conical hills, ridges, ravines, spires, pinnacles and hundreds of other strange forms weathered by wind and rain. It is one of the world's most astonishing examples of erosion, and many of the formations are tinted in various colors. The area has been a virtual goldmine for fossil remains of prehistoric animals.

The steeply eroded landscape supports little animal life except for swifts, cliff swallows, rock wrens, prairie dogs, badgers, coyotes, porcupines, chipmunks, jackrabbits, snakes and bison.

French-Canadian trappers in search of beaver to the west were the first men to record their impressions of the badlands. They described the region appropriately as *les mauvaises terres à traverser*— 'bad lands to travel across.' The Indians in the area called it *mako sica*—'bad land.'

Badlands, with its 243,302 acres (380 square miles) was made a national monument by President Franklin D Roosevelt in 1939 and became Badlands National Park in 1978.

*Below*: **A morning view of the Pinnacles in Badlands National Park. Nearby is the herd of some 300 buffalo in the Sage Creek region.**

# BIG BEND

B ig Bend National Park is located south of Alpine, Texas, and it includes the state's largest wilderness. In it are the Chisos Mountains, with their rugged rock formations and pinnacles; the dramatic Santa Elena, Boquillas and Mariscal Canyons, formed by the Rio Grande; Chisos Basin, the most developed part of the park.

The Indians said that after making the earth, the Great Spirit simply dumped all the leftover rocks on the Big Bend. Spanish explorers, less familiar with the landscape, merely called the area 'the uninhabited land.'

The park, with its 708,118 acres (1106 square miles) is the home of cactus, juniper, piñon oak, ponderosas, Douglas fir, Arizona cypress, quaking aspen, deer, coyotes, peccaries, and over 400 bird species. Mexican mountain ranges such as the Sierra del Carmen can be seen from the park, which was authorized in 1935. The name, Big Bend, refers to the giant U-turn the Rio Grande makes here in Southwest Texas along the border with Mexico.

*Above*: **Sunrise in Santa Elena Canyon; the Rio Grande flows through Big Bend National Park. The deep rock strata of Santa Elena shows the vast reaches of time in this area, which is a part of the mountains called Sierra de Santa Elena, stretching into Mexico. Prehistoric Indians made their homes here at least 10,000 years ago and perhaps earlier, but little evidence of human occupation appears until the Archaic or Desert Culture of 6000 BC. These people were not farmers, but hunters and gatherers, taking only what this country offered on its own.**

*Right*: **Looking down-river from the mouth of the Santa Elena Canyon in Big Bend National Park. The steep rock faces are part of the Sierra Ponce. The park is 97 percent desert and at midday in the summer, the ground temperature may reach 180°F, and it can be freezing cold in winter when a northern storm sweeps through. But it also can be a mild 80°F while the Rocky Mountains are locked in deep snow.**

# BISCAYNE

Biscayne National Park, established in 1980, is a wonderland at the northern end of the Florida Keys. The greater part of the park's 172,845 acres (270 square miles) is water and reef. Here can be gained an understanding of a complex and fascinating geologic-biologic process—the building of a coral reef. These reefs owe their existence to groups of animals and plants that deposit calcium around themselves as a protective shell. As millions and millions of these living things attach themselves, lay down their deposits and die, the reef grows. The area was a home for pirates in the old days, and the waters of the park contain several shipwrecks as reminders.

*Right*: **Biscayne National Park is a nature lover's paradise.**

*Below*: **An aerial view of Adam's Key in Biscayne National Park. It is separated from Elliot Key by very shallow water.**

# BRYCE CANYON

Bryce Canyon National Park, near St George, Utah, is a spectacularly colorful and unusual example of the effects of erosion by water. Its tinted, odd-shaped rock formations, petrified logs and the Grosvenor Natural Bridge are wonders to behold. The many shapes and forms of these phenomena conjure up all sorts of images: walls and windows, minarets, gables, pagodas and pedestals, temples and even 'platoons of Turkish soldiers in pantaloons.' The red rocks of the park were deposited by vast lakes that once covered the area. In earlier times dinosaurs tramped its swamps, foraging tons of plant food and leaving their story in fossil bones.

By the time that Paiute Indians moved into the area, living conditions were considerably tougher. Their name for Bryce Canyon translates as 'Red rocks standing like men in a bowl-shaped canyon.' But they did attach spiritual values to the other-worldly canyon. Mormon settler Ebeneezer Bryce lived there for five years, trying to make a go of the land. He gave his name to the place and his description of it still survives: 'A hell of a place to lose a cow.'

The forest and meadows of Bryce Canyon support a remarkable diversity of animal life, including some 164 species of birds. The 35,835 acre (56 square miles) park was authorized in 1924.

*Below*: **Limestone features in Queen's Garden, Bryce Canyon National Park, looking from Sunset Point, located in the Bryce Amphitheater section of the park. The color comes from the oxidation of minerals, especially iron.**

*Overleaf*: **The Navajo Loop Trail in Bryce Canyon after a January snowstorm. The trail begins at Sunset Point and is one and a half miles long, but it may take one and a half hours because of its 521-foot ascent.**

*Above*: A view of Silent City from Inspiration Point in Bryce Canyon. Boat Mesa in background.

# CANYONLANDS

Canyonlands National Park, with its 337,570 acres (527 square miles) was established in 1964. Located near Moab, Utah, the park is distinguished by high cliffs, buttes and mesas of various shades of red, with the lush banks of the Colorado and Green Rivers below—some of the most breathtaking scenery in the West. The park also contains the Natural Bridges National Monument, with its three natural stone bridges; and Hovenweep National Monument, with its six groups of ancient structures built by Pueblo Indians more than 800 years ago.

This is desert country. It looks desolate and empty, but actually a wide variety of plant and animal life thrives. Bighorn sheep, mule deer, cougars, bobcats, coyotes, foxes and pronghorn can be found here, as well as small mammals, rodents and some reptiles. The birdlife is quite varied, and in recent years formerly unknown species of flowers, insects and microscopic animals have been discovered here.

*Right*: **The north section of Canyonlands National park.**
*Below*: **A view of Sandstone Rim in Shafer Canyon from Island in the Sky, whose elevation is approximately 6000 feet.**

# CAPITOL REEF

Capitol Reef National Park, near Price, Utah, has an area of 241,904 acres (378 square miles), and was established in 1971. Capitol Reef itself is a 75-mile long sandstone cliff with dome-shaped formations. Capitol Gorge, one of the most outstanding formations in the park, is a deep narrow canyon with Basket-maker period Indian petroglyphs about half way down on the north wall. A short trail leads to the scenic Hickman Natural Bridge. The park also features the cliff-enclosed Fremont River and Cohab Canyon. Capitol Dome resembles the dome of the Capitol Building in Washington, DC.

The rock in Canyonlands was laid down, layer upon layer, over a period of millions of years. At times the area was a tidal flat whose ripple marks have now hardened into stone. At other times sand dunes drifted across the land, and they were eventually consolidated into criss-crossing beds of sandstone. The park presents a wonderful contrast between the fertile growth along the Fremont River and the barrenness of the cliffs and terraces. Though the Fremont River is an oasis, there is abundant life in other, drier parts of the park. Piñon pine and Utah juniper trees, which are well adapted for living in a dry climate, jut unexpectedly into the landscape. Animals can be found, too—side-blotched lizards, antelope squirrel, canyon wren, bats, chipmunks, ringtail cats, foxes, mountain lions and deer.

The Fremont Indians lived here for about 400 years, beginning at approximately 800 AD. Their petroglyphs still elude translation, but the figures of people and bighorn sheep seem to depict hunting. These Indians hunted, gathered wild foods and farmed. Later Paiute Indians hunted game and gathered plant foods in Capitol Reef. In 1880 Mormon settlers arrived, establishing the town, Fruita, where the park campgrounds are located today.

*Below*: **Sunset at the Temple of the Sun and the Temple of the Moon in the Cathedral Valley section of Capitol Reef National Park.**

*Below right*: **The lush valley of the Fremont River near Fruita, the Mormon town. This is also the area where the Indians grew their crops.**

*Overleaf*: **Capitol Reef National Park is far from being a total desert, as these green grasses and beautiful red cactus blossoms will attest.**

*Overleaf inset*: **The upper Cathedral Valley in the afternoon sun. These upthrusts of sedimentary rock layers were caused by pressures generated from the formation of the Rocky Mountain Chain.**

# CARLSBAD CAVERNS

Carlsbad Caverns National Park was established in 1930, and its 46,755 acres (73 square miles) contain the earth's largest known cavern—it still has not been fully explored. Located in the foothills of the Guadalupe Mountains southwest of Carlsbad, New Mexico, the cavern contains—in addition to several smaller caves—prehistoric Indian sites and portions of pioneer trails, limestone stalagmites, stalactites, helictites and other formations begun more than 60 million years ago.

It has 23 miles of explored passageways and chambers; about three miles are open to visitors. Scientists have explored down to 1100 feet, but tourists go only to the 829–foot level.

A magnificent huge natural arch forms the entrance, some 40 feet high and 90 feet wide. Inside, the cavern temperature is a constant 56 degrees Fahrenheit.

For thousands of years, bats that winter in Mexico have used one portion of the main cavern as a summer home. From late spring until the first frost in October or early November, these tiny flying mammals become the big tourist attraction as they wing their way out of the cavern in search of food. Their numbers are incredible as they exit at sunset each evening,

*Below*: **Inside the Carlsbad Caverns. The limestone in which the caverns formed was deposited about 250 million years ago.**

# CHANNEL ISLANDS

Channel Islands National Park, with its 249,354 acres (390 square miles) of territory near Ventura, California, was established in 1980. The park includes five of a chain of eight islands in the Pacific Ocean, and can be reached only by boat. Even the visitor center is located on the mainland.

Anacapa Island (actually a slender chain of narrow islands) in spring is a riot of color, with its overwhelming wildflower display. California sea lions and harbor seals can be seen along the rocky shores. In January and March, the annual migration of gray whales passes nearby.

Santa Barbara Island has steep cliffs—some of them 500 feet high—and caves, coves, offshore pillars and blowholes. Sea mammals, including the huge elephant seal, can be seen.

San Miguel Island could be the setting for a science fiction movie because of its 'caliches' or 'fossil forests.' It also is the only place in the world where as many as six species of seals and sea lions can be found.

Santa Rosa and Santa Cruz Islands are unusual in that even though they are a part of the park, they are privately-owned.

*Top*: **Morning at Inspiration Point, East Anacapa Island, the largest of the three Anacapa Islands. For much of the year, Anacapa looks brown and lifeless, but with the advent of the winter rains, the island's plants emerge from their summer dormancy and again turn green. In the spring the flowers burst forth with their blooms.**
*Right*: **The moon at sunrise over the Channel Islands National Park. Because the rocks and depressions are exposed to air and drowned by water twice each day, their life forms are those which can live in both worlds.**

# CRATER LAKE

Crater Lake National Park contains an extraordinary blue lake in the crater of an extinct volcano encircled by lava walls from 500 to 2000 feet high. Established in 1902, the park encompasses 160,290 acres (250 square miles) near Klamath Falls, Oregon. Crater Lake is in the heart of the Cascade Range of mountains (which also includes Mount Rainier and Mount St Helens) and nearby, in this superbly wooded area, are peaks rising to more than 8000 feet, guarding the unique and incredibly blue jewel of the lake itself. The lake surface is more than 6000 feet above sea level, and its shining waters are some 1932 feet deep.

Fiery avalanches sometimes interrupted the lives of the Indians who lived near Mount Mazama some 6000 years ago. The Indians believed that Mazama's violent eruptions (before its collapse) were the result of a war between two gods, Llao and Skell. Their shamans forbade most Indians from viewing the resulting lake, and the Indians did not mention the lake to pioneers who criss–crossed the area for 50 years without discovering it. In 1853, while searching for the Lost Cabin Gold Mine, a small party of prospectors, including John Wesley Hillman, accidentally discovered Crater Lake.

But the credit for making it a national park area goes to William Gladstone Steel. As a Kansas schoolboy, he read of Crater Lake in a newspaper used to wrap his school lunch. When he first saw the lake, his commitment to visit it became a pledge to preserve this natural wonder somehow. Steel lobbied for 17 years for it to be made a national park. His perseverance paid off on 22 May 1902. On that day Crater Lake was established as a national park by the United States Federal Government.

*Above*: A view of Eagle Crags and the Phantom Ship Formation on the southeast edge of Crater Lake. The reason that the water is so blue is that light is absorbed color by color as it passes through clear water. First the red goes, then orange, yellow and green. The last to be absorbed is the blue. Only the deepest blue gets reflected back to the surface from 300 feet, the natural limit of penetration. Then it is seen as the color of the water. Actually the water is no more blue that the sky is blue.

*Left*: Another view of the Phantom Ship formation in Crater Lake—this time from the Sun Notch on Mount Thielsen at sunset.

*Opposite far left*: A winter view of Wizard Island in Crater Lake. Wizard Island is actually a small extinct volcanic cone that built up after Mount Mazama collapsed to form the caldera in which Crater Lake and the island are located.

# DENALI

Denali National Park, near Fairbanks, Alaska, is huge, containing 4,700,000 acres (7344 square miles). It lies in the Alaska Range, and includes the towering Mount McKinley, the tallest mountain on the North American Continent, with a height of 20,320 feet. Established in 1917 as Mount McKinley National Park, its name was changed to Denali National Park on 2 December 1980. At that time, the boundaries of the former park were enlarged by some four million acres (6250 square miles), making it slightly larger than Massachusetts. The name, Denali, was what Athabascan Indians called the mountain.

Denali National Park and Preserve is managed as three distinct units. Denali Wilderness, the former Mount McKinley National Park, is managed to maintain the accessible but undeveloped wilderness parkland character. Denali National Park (excluding Denali Wilderness) allows subsistence hunting and trapping by local rural residents. This recognizes a long–standing dependence on wildlife, fish and plants for subsistence. Denali National Preserve allows the same uses as Denali National Park and also allows sport hunting, trapping and fishing.

*Right*: **More than 430 species of flowering plants, as well as mosses, lichens, fungi and algae, grace the slopes and valleys of the Denali National Park, but they can all stand the subarctic.**
*Below*: **The Polychrome Glacier on the east fork of the Toklat River, photographed from Polychrome Mountain in the Denali National Park—one of the many glaciers in the area.**

*Above*: Mount McKinley in the morning, looking from the north. The mountain was named for the president from Ohio, William McKinley, and crowns the 600-mile long Alaska Range.

# EVERGLADES

Everglades National Park, in southern Florida, near Florida City, is not a swamp, although there are some swampy areas. The Indians called this 1,398,800 acre (2186 square miles) region 'River of Grass,' an appropriate term because, over most of the Everglades, water moves slowly southward to the Gulf of Mexico and Florida Bay like a shallow river. Sometimes it is concealed by tall grasses and hammocks of cypress and mangrove.

Everglades National Park, which encompasses most of the state of Florida south of Miami, was authorized in 1934, and contains the largest remaining subtropical wilderness in the continental United States. The region, which begins near Lake Okeechobee and Palmdale and extends to the Gulf, might be compared to the shallow bowl of a gigantic spoon. The rim consists of ridges of limestone, wider on the east coast than on the west coast.

Along these ridges, coastal resorts have been built. Between them, the land drains from the area of Lake Okeechobee, toward the point of the spoon, into a maze of waterways and marshes which shred the southwestern coast.

The alligator is the best–known Everglades denizen, but the park contains hundreds of species of animals, many of them exotic. Here can be found the manatee (or sea cow), the Florida panther (or cougar), the green sea turtle and the crocodile, among others.

But the Everglades is best known for its abundance and variety of birdlife. There are ospreys, great white herons, brown pelicans, wood storks, southern bald eagles, anhingas, roseate spoonbills, flamingos, egrets, Florida sandhill cranes, Everglades kites, short-tailed hawks, peregrine falcons and Cape Sable sparrows. Some of the animal life is on the endangered species list.

*Below*: **Sunset over the Everglades in a spot that could not possibly be mistaken for a swamp. It is a freshwater river six inches deep and 50 miles wide that creeps seaward through the Everglades on a riverbed that slopes ever so gradually. Along its course the water drops 15 feet.**

*Opposite*: **Shark valley in Everglades National Park. Here may be seen a variety of wildlife that inhabits the wide shallow waterway which eventually empties into Shark River. Alligators, otters, snakes, turtles and birds, including rare wood storks and the Everglades kite, are natives.**

# GATES OF THE ARCTIC

***Above*: A bull caribou on the tundra in Gates of the Arctic National Park in Alaska.**

***Right*: the Arctic Tundra in Gates of the Arctic Natonal Park does provide some food for caribou and other ungulates.**

Gates of the Arctic National Park, a 7,500,000 acre (11,719 square miles) area, was established in 1980 and is located in the north central region of Alaska, about 200 miles northwest of Fairbanks. Spectacular in size, peaks of granite and sharp ridges are bisected by splendid long valleys, many of them containing glittering lakes and sparkling rivers in this wilderness area. It is the second largest national park in the world, Wrangell–St Elias National Park in southeastern Alaska being the biggest, and the entire park is located above the Arctic Circle.

Its name was given to it by Robert Marshall, a scientist, explorer and conservationist, who was conducting research near the headwaters of the Koyukuk River from 1929 to 1939. He came upon two peaks facing each other, which he christened Frigid Crags and Boreal, and together named them Gates of the Arctic. He was the one who asked that the 600–mile long Brooks Range, extending from the Yukon to the Arctic Sea, be established as a federal wilderness area.

For centuries the Eskimos have hunted here for the great Western Arctic caribou, whose huge herds migrate hundreds of miles per year, passing back and forth through the passes from northern calving grounds and feeding ranges south of the mountains. Black bear, Dall sheep, moose, wolverines, lynx, grizzly bear, eagles, falcons and many migratory birds also live or visit here.

# GLACIER

Glacier National Park in Montana, along the Canadian border, is located near West Glacier. Established in 1910, the park measures 1,013,595 acres (1584 square miles) and contains superb Rocky Mountain scenery, numerous glaciers and glacial lakes. Since 1932 it has been a part of Waterton–Glacier International Peace Park along with the Canadian National Park, Waterton Lakes, located just above the border.

The park was named for the more than 50 glaciers that are found there. These beds of ice are the remains of a large system of mountain glaciers that covered the area at one time. Some of them are only a few acres in size, but others are very large, such as Blackfoot Glacier, the largest in the park, which covers three square miles.

The park is also noted for its mountains, the highest of which is Mount Cleveland, rising to a height of 10,438 feet. Other mountains higher than 10,000 feet are Kintla Peak, Mount Siyehand and Mount Stimson. There are also some 250 lakes inside the park—the most beautiful being the Upper Saint Mary,

*Below*: **Lake McDonald in Glacier National Park, the largest lake in the park. Measuring 11 miles in length, it averages a width of one and a half miles. It has heavily-forested shores and the peaks nearby rise 6000 feet above the surface.**

Logan pass in Glacier National Park, with beautiful
wildflowers and magnificent mountain peaks.

# GLACIER BAY

Glacier Bay National Park was established in 1980 and contains an area of 3,225,197 acres (5039 square miles). The park, which had been a national monument from 1925 to 1980, is located about 75 miles from Juneau, Alaska. Of the vast glaciers in Alaska which extend themselves and creep toward the sea, the largest and most majestic clusters of them are located in this park. It is here where the huge Muir Glacier, two miles wide and 250 feet thick, is found. These glaciers slowly move down from a vast icecap among 15,000–foot peaks into a fiord 60 miles long and two miles wide on their way to the sea.

Many species of animals have been able to combat the unfriendly climate. Among them are black bears, brown bears, river otters, mink, mountain goats, marmots, shrews, mice, moose and coyotes. In the watery areas of the park have been found humpback whales, killer whales, Dall porpoises and harbor porpoises. Harbor seals select densely packed icebergs at the face of both the Muir and the Johns Hopkins Glaciers for their pupping grounds.

*Right*: **Icebergs stranded on the beach at low tide in Glacier Bay.**

*Below*: **A view of Riggs Glacier, which empties into the Muir Inlet leading to Glacier Bay.**

# GRAND CANYON

Grand Canyon National Park is located in the most spectacular part of the Colorado River's greatest canyon. Established in 1908, it covers 1,218,375 acres (1904 square miles) in northwestern Arizona. John Muir, the famous American naturalist, said of it in 1898: 'The Grand Canyon of the Colorado . . . as unearthly in the color and grandeur and quantity of its architecture as if you had found it after death on some other star.' Major John Wesley Powell, a one–armed veteran of the Civil War, led the first expedition down the Colorado River through the Grand Canyon. He rode the river in a chair strapped to one of the group's wooden boats and searched the river ahead for hidden rocks and rapids. This adventurous geologist also gave the canyon its name when he referred to it in his diary as the Grand Canyon as he related the story of that 1869 trip.

Powell, however, was not the first white man to discover the canyon, since Spaniards from Coronado's expedition discovered it in 1540. But ruins of adobe houses in the Grand Canyon show that Pueblo Indians lived in this area, probably as early as the 1200s.

The Colorado River at the bottom of the canyon rushes along about 1850 feet above sea level. Rocks, cliffs, hills, ridges and valleys of every form prise the sides of the canyon. Many of the ridges have weather–carved lines which make them resemble Chinese temples. Thick forests cover the canyon rims. The North Rim of the Grand Canyon rises about 1200 feet higher than the South Rim. The highest points on the rim are about 9000 feet above sea level, or 7150 feet above the river—more than a mile.

**At sunset the structures in Grand Canyon National Park can take on beautiful pastel shades. This is a view from Maricopa Point on the South Rim, which is near the rim worship site, the village amphitheater, the visitor center, the Powell Memorial and the Bright Angel Lodge.**

**The Grand Canyon is a product of the conflict between two great earth forces: mountain–building on the one hand and gravity on the other. This portion of the earth's crust has been elevated one and a half miles above sea level, and the river, powered by gravity, has cut through it.**

*Top*: Buckwheat growing on a ledge on Cape Royal on the North Rim at the bottom of the Walhala Plateau.

*Above*: A twilight view of some more ledges at Bright Angel Point on the North Rim near the Grand Canyon Lodge.

*Left*: A panoramic view of the stately Grand Canyon.

*Overleaf*: Mather Point on the south rim of the Grand Canyon.

# GRAND TETON

Grand Teton National Park, near Jackson, Wyoming, was established in 1929 and covers 310,516 acres (485 square miles). It includes some of the most breathtaking landscape in North America. Within the park are the alpine–like, glacier–carved Grand Teton Mountains with their jagged horn–like peaks and intervening canyons; a dozen glaciers; eight large lakes; extensive fir, spruce and pine forests and summits ranging from 11,000 to nearly 14,000 feet above sea level. It its also the winter feeding ground for the largest American elk herd.

All of Grand Teton is a sanctuary in which many animals can be found, including elk, mule deer, bison, moose, chipmunks, golden–mantled ground squirrel, pikas (or 'cony'), marmots, beavers, bighorn sheep, pronghorns, trumpeter swans, eagles, woodpeckers, marsh hawks, sage grouse and other animals.

A stroll along the valley floor or on one of the trails into the high country can take the plant lover through forests of lodgepole pine, Englemann spruce, limber pines, white–bark pines, alpine fir and Douglas fir. Cottonwoods grow in profusion along the streams, together with willows and aspens—important food for moose and beaver. In the valley and on intermediate terrain are stands of sagebrush, in open or unforested sites, silverberry bushes glistening on the sandbars, and creeping mahonia with prickly, holly-like leaves.

Around Jackson Lake can be found displays of geranium, scarlet gilia, balsamroot, blue lupine, larkspur, fleabane, penstemons, and cream-colored clusters of wild buckwheat. A flower that can hardly be missed is the Indian paintbrush, which is Wyoming's state flower.

*Below*: **Sunrise over the Tetons in Grand Teton National Park. A view from Schwabacher Landing on the Snake River.**

**Grand Teton National Park is filled with beautiful trees, spectacular groups of wildlife and the grandeur of the mountains.**

*Above*: Mount St John in the Teton Range in Grand Teton National Park. A morning view looking across Jackson Lake.

*Right*: A morning shot of String Lake with the mountains in the background. String Lake is actually not a lake at all; it is more like a natural passageway between Leigh Lake and Jenny Lake.

*Far right*: Snake River, which flows from the north to Jackson Lake and then exits the lake near its southern end, bisects the Grand Tetons National Park. Here it is seen on a September morning.

# GREAT SMOKY MOUNTAINS

Great Smoky Mountains National Park, authorized in 1926, covers 520,269 acres (813 square miles), and straddles the North Carolina-Tennessee border. The Smoky Mountains, themselves, constitute the largest mountain range in the eastern United States, and the park is filled with magnificent virgin forests.

The park, which represents the majestic climax of the Appalachian Highlands, is a woodlands sanctuary preserving the world's finest examples of temperate deciduous forest. The name *Smoky* comes from the smoke–like haze enveloping the mountains, which stretches in sweeping troughs and mighty billows to the horizon. The park boasts unspoiled forests similar to those that the early pioneers found. Restored log cabins and barns stand as reminders of those who carved a living from this wilderness.

Fertile soils and abundant rain have encouraged the development of a world–renowned variety of flora, including more than 1400 kinds of flowering plants. More than 800 miles of trails thread by its waterfalls, coves and rushing streams.

*Top*: Cades Cove in the Great Smoky Mountains National Park. This is an outdoor museum on the Tennessee side of the park that, in addition to the splendid scenery, features log cabins, barns, and a waterwheel that still powers gristmill.

*Left*: Fall colors in October in the Great Smoky Mountains National Park.

*Next page*: A scene of moss–covered rocks and waterfalls in the Great Smoky Mountains National Park.

# GUADALUPE

Guadalupe Mountains National Park is located on the Texas side of the Texas–New Mexico border, and adjoins Carlsbad Caverns National Park. Authorized in 1966 and containing 76,293 acres (119 square miles), it is really an extensive Permian limestone fossil reef that contains a tremendous earth fault. These mountains stand like an island in the desert, silent sentinels watching over the most extensive fossil reef complex known to man. The rocks which make up the Guadalupe Mountains were formed 225 to 280 million years ago. An inland sea which covered more than 10,000 square miles of Texas and New Mexico controlled their formation.

The mountain range resembles a massive wedge—rising in Texas, its arms reach northward into New Mexico. At its 'V' stands El Capitan, a 2000–foot sheer cliff. The mountains and canyons shelter a unique remnant of forest plants and animals which have struggled for survival since the end of the Ice Age about 10,000 years ago.

Animals commonly seen here include elk, mule deer, wild turkey, raccoon, porcupine, kit and gray foxes and coyote. Black bear and cougar pay occasional visits. More than 200 species of birds and 52 species of reptiles and amphibians have been identified in the park.

In the sheltered canyons where moisture is more abundant, ferns, big–tooth maple, chokecherry, walnut, hophornbeam, Texas madrone and other species of plants appear. In the desert area there are such plants as creosotebush, lechuguilla, Parry agave, yucca and sotol. The high country has a forest of ponderosa pine, Douglas fir, limber pine. A few aspens survive as a reminder of a forest that covered this area thousands of years ago, when the climate was cooler and the rainfall greater.

For the past 12,000 years the mountain caves, springs, plants and wildlife provided shelter and sustenance to various groups of people. Spanish *conquistadores* passed nearby on trips from Mexico in the 1500s and found Mescalero Apaches there. Surveyors mapping a route to California in 1849 passed near El Capitan. Shortly after the Civil War, ranching activities began and the area was settled. At times the settlers had to contend with outlaws, cattle rustlers and Apache raiders. In the 1870s soldiers from nearby military posts camped at Pine Springs while trying to subdue the remaining Apaches and move them to a reservation.

**El Capitan at sunrise, looking from the southeast. It was in the shallow water of a vast inland sea that the Capitan reef was built by lime–secreting algae and other organisms. As the reef grew upward and seaward upon talus broken loose by storms, sediments were also deposited in a lagoon between the reef and the land.**

# HALEAKALA

Haleakala National Park, authorized in 1960, covers 28,655 acres (45 square miles), and contains Mount Haleakala, a 10,023–foot dormant volcano. Located on the Island of Maui, the crater of the volcano is a cool, cone–studded reminder of past activity. Streaks of red, yellow, gray and black trace the courses of recent and ancient lava, ash and cinder flows. The volcanic rocks slowly break down as natural forces reduce them to minute particles which are swept away by wind, heavy rain and intermittent streams.

The Island of Maui itself began as two separate volcanoes on the ocean floor. Time and time again, eon after eon, they erupted until the volcano heads emerged from the sea.

Legend has it that Hina, mother of the demigod Maui, had trouble drying her bark cloth because the day was too short. So Maui went to the great mountain that the sun passed over each day and, as the sun's rays crept over the mountain, snared them and held them fast with his ropes. 'Give me my life,' pleaded the sun. 'I will give you your life,' said Maui, 'If you promise to go more slowly across the sky.' And to this day the sun is careful to go slowly across the heavens, and the great mountain is known as Haleakala: The House of the Sun.

Several hundred years have passed since the last volcanic activity occurred within the crater, but there were two minor lava flows in 1790 which altered the southwest coastline.

**The Haleakala Crater. Years ago, when volcanic activity occurred near the summit, lava poured down the stream valleys, nearly filling them. More recently, cinders, ash, volcanic bombs and spatter were blown from the numberous young vents in the crater, forming multicolored symmetrical cones as high as 600 feet. Thus this water–carved basin became partially filled with lava and cinder cones, and it then came to resemble a true volcanic crater in every respect.**

# HAWAII VOLCANOES

Hawaii Volcanoes National Park is on the Island of Hawaii and contains the active volcanoes Kilauea (4077 feet) and Mauna Loa (13,680 feet). Indeed, Mauna Loa erupted as recently as 25 March 1984 with its most intense lava flow since 1950. Kilauea followed suit on 30 March. The park, established in 1916, has an area of 229,177 acres (358 square miles).

The Hawaii Volcanoes National Park is a botanist's paradise. Of the more than 1700 plant species to be found there, at least 98 percent grow only in the Hawaiian Islands. Botanists believe that all of the 1700 species evolved from a small number of ancestors, probably fewer than 250 seeds or tiny plants. Among the better known examples of Hawaii's endemic plants are the splendid acacia koa, the tree lobelias and the shrubby violets.

*Left*: **Mount Kilauea in the Hawaii Volcanoes National Park spews lava into the air during its eruption of March 1983—just one year before the famous March 1984 eruption of nearby Mauna Loa.**

*Following page*: **The Ohia Tree Fern Forest in the Kilauea Caldera. A caldera is a crater formed by the collapse of the central part of a volcano or by explosions of extraordinary violence.**

# ISLE ROYALE

Isle Royale National Park is located in Lake Superior off the coast of the State of Michigan. Authorized in 1931, it is an island wilderness of hardwood forests with an area of 571,790 acres (893 square miles), making it the largest island in Lake Superior.

Long before Europeans saw Isle Royale, Indians mined copper there. Using hand–held beach cobbles, they hammered out chunks of pure copper from the hard bedrock. Archaeologists have excavated their shallow mining pits, some dating back 4500 years. The French claimed possession of the island in 1671. In 1783 it became a US possession, and was identified as Chippewa Territory until 1843. Modern copper mining was carried on between the mid–1880s and 1899, and during that time large areas were burned, the forest was logged and settlements developed.

The 1830s saw the advent of commercial fishing, and the American Fur Company gill–netted whitefish, lake trout and siskiwit. Early in this century Isle Royale became popular for summer homes, excursions and as a wilderness retreat. It was Detroit journalist Albert Stoll who sparked the fight to make it a national park.

Sometime early in this century, moose immigrated to the island, probably swimming from Canada's mainland. By the early 1930s the moose, with no natural enemies, had destroyed their food supply and began to die in great numbers. During the cold winter of 1948–49 an ice bridge formed between Canada and the island, and a small pack of Eastern Timber Wolves crossed to Isle Royale. Now, the wolves take moose—the very old, the very young, the sick and the injured—thus maintaining a healthy moose population.

*Above*: **Mott Island, located to the far southeast of Isle Royale National Park. It is here where the park headquarters are located.**
*Right*: **A view of the forests of Isle Royale National Park. Some 10,000 years ago the island appeared beneath glacial ice, rising as the level of Lake Superior dropped. The island developed soil and was colonized by plants and animals. Its many inland lakes first formed in basins gouged out by glaciers, and then began to shrink, as lakes and ponds inevitably do. But the ridge-and-trough pattern of the rocks is the work of millions of years, pre–dating even the formation of Lake Superior. Isle Royale is indeed an island of superlatives in wilderness and beauty.**

# KINGS CANYON

Kings Canyon National Park, established in 1940, is located in east–central California and contains 460,136 acres (719 square miles). It is a mountain wilderness, dominated by the Kings River and the High Sierra Mountains, but its main attractions are the giant sequoia trees— some of the oldest and largest in the United States.

The Grant Grove section of the park has trees that are 2000 to 3000 years old, and the largest and most famous of those is the General Grant, which is 267 feet high, with a base circumference of 108 feet. So big is it that it has been named 'The Nation's Christmas Tree.' Another giant in the grove is the General Lee Tree, the second largest in the grove. In addition to the sequoias, the park has many huge pine trees.

Northeast of Grant Grove is the Kings River portion of the park. There the winding Kings River carves out Tehipite Valley Canyon and Kings Canyon. Kings Canyon is about ten miles long and one–half mile wide, with walls 2500 to 5000 feet high. Snow–capped mountains tower above the canyons, and much of the park can be reached only by trail. The park is located several miles east of Fresno, and borders on Sequoia National Park. They are virtually a single park and are administrated as such.

*Above right*: **An afternoon view of Rae Lakes in Kings Canyon Natonal Park, in the Sierra Nevada Mountains. Dragon Peak is to the left and Painted Lady Peak is to the right.**

*Right*: **A wilderness camp at Rae Lakes in the Sierra Nevada, Kings Canyon National Park. The spot is located just north of Kearsage Pass, which has an elevation of 11,823 feet.**

*Opposite*: **A summer morning view of Roaring River Falls on the South Fork of Kings Canyon. This is near the highest canyon wall in the US—a sheer 8350-foot rise from the river to the top of Spanish Mountain.**

# KOBUK VALLEY

Kobuk Valley National Park in Alaska is one of the newest of the national parks, having been established in 1980. But it is huge, covering 1,750,000 acres (2734 square miles). It is in a wilderness and is practically inaccessible except for by small aircraft. The nearest community is Kotzebue, an old Eskimo community.

Some 40 miles above the Arctic Circle, the park contains the Great Kobuk Sand Dunes which cover 25 square miles, and may rise to a height of 100 feet. Despite its dry, cold climate, Kobuk is the summer breeding place for more than 100 species of birds. In addition to the thousands of caribou traveling between northern calving and southern wintering grounds, the foraging territory here is shared with such animals of the North as grizzly bear, black bear, wolf and fox.

**Ahnewetut Creek cuts through the Great Kobuk Sand Dunes in Kobuk National Park, Alaska. These sand dunes can be reached on an easy hike from the Kobuk River.**

# LAKE CLARK

Lake Clark National Park is another huge Alaskan national park, occupying 2,874,000 acres (4491 square miles) across the Cook Inlet from Anchorage. Established in 1980 it is a scenic wilderness rich in fish and wildlife. The Alaska and Aleutian Ranges of mountains join here, and between them stand the awesome Chigmit Mountains, formed by violent earth movement and sculpted by glaciers.

Access to the Lake Clark region is almost exclusively by small aircraft, and no highways lead into it. In some locations, the winter sun does not rise above the peaks for several months. The snow and ice breakup in spring can immobilize the area, as ice and snow melt and frozen ground turns to mud. But in the summer, all changes. Caribou calve, buds turn to leaves, mosquitoes hatch, and salmon return to spawn. Everywhere, the rain produces a summer floral display. Fireweed, lupine, blueberry and boarberry abound. In the autumn the burgundy–hued tundra is beautiful, especially around the aptly–named Turquoise Lake.

The area has been occupied by humans since prehistoric times, and is an archeological treasure trove.

*Right*: **A river in Lake Clark National Park, with the peaks of the Chigmit Mountains in the distance. In the foreground is a part of the Arctic tundra, a region where the richly hued terrain may support stands of boreal spruce trees.**

*Below*: **A July scene on Turquoise Lake—six-week-old moose calves explore the lake shore. In the waters of the park can be found salmon, rainbow trout, Dolly Varden, lake trout, northern pike and Arctic grayling.**

# LASSEN VOLCANIC

Lassen Volcanic National Park, established in 1916, covers 106,372 acres (166 square miles) near Redding, in northeastern California, and contains Lassen Peak, a 10,466-foot high volcano, which erupted intermittently from 1914 to 1921. Hardened lava from these eruptions covers its slopes, and hot springs flow from its south side.

In the northwest section of the park the Chaos region has hundreds of steep domes of lava that were pushed up from below the earth's surface, forming odd-looking formations called Chaos Crags and Chaos Jumbles. More than 40 glacier-made lakes can be found in the park, including Reflection Lake, which mirrors Lassen Peak. Three large lakes called the Chain-of-Lakes lie in the eastern part of the park, while hot springs bubble on the surface of Boiling Spring Lake.

This national park supports some 50 kinds of mammals, 150 kinds of birds and about 12 different kinds of reptiles and amphibians. Plant life includes conifers, such as pines, firs and cedars; broadleaf trees, such as aspens and cottonwoods, willows and alders; and many kinds of wildflowers.

The great mass of Lassen Peak began as stiff, pasty lava forced from a vent on the north slope of a larger extinct volcano known as Tehama. The lava was squeezed up to form a rough, dome-shaped mass, plugging the vent from which it came. After this plug dome was formed, Lassen Peak was calm until 30 May 1914. Then it did not stop erupting for seven years.

*Below*: **Lassen Peak, with Manzanita Lake in the foreground. The lake is near the northwest boundary of the park.**

*Right*: **Lassen Peak with Hat Creek in the foreground. There are some 150 miles of foot trails in the park.**

# MESA VERDE

Mesa Verde National Park contains the most notable and best preserved prehistoric cliff dwellings in the United States, including homes and temples. Established in 1906, it covers 52,085 acres (81 square miles) in Colorado, between Cortez and Durango. These well–preserved cliff dwellings, tucked among the canyon walls, are located in a huge, steep–sided tableland interlaced with canyons and crowned with thick piñon and juniper woods.

Here may be traced four cultural periods: the Basket Makers (1–450 AD); the Modified Basket Makers (450–750 AD), which brought the bow and arrow, pottery and houses; Development Pueblo Period (750–1100 AD), with kivas and sturdier structures; and the Great or Classic Pueblo Period (1100–1300 AD), during which the impressive cliff homes were built, and arts and crafts reached their peaks of development.

The people who lived here during the two Pueblo Periods are called the Anasazi, from a Navajo word meaning 'the ancient ones.' They were a Stone Age people, without metal of any kind, but they skillfully shaped stone, bone and wood into a variety of tools.

*Top*: **The Cliff Palace on a July morning. This was the first major dwelling to be discovered in Mesa Verde National Park. It was found by local cowboys about a century ago, and contains more than 200 living rooms, 23 kivas (kiva is a Hopi word for 'ceremonial room') and numerous storage rooms.**

*Right*: **A panoramic shot of the Cliff Palace, which was probably built during the middle decades of the 1200s. Many rooms were plastered and decorated with painted designs.**

# MOUNT RAINIER

Mount Rainier National Park is one of the oldest parks in the system — dating back to 1899. Located in the State of Washington, southeast of Tacoma, it covers 235,404 acres (368 square miles). It contains, in addition to the majestic and inspiring Mount Rainier itself, the greatest single–peak glacier system in the lower 48 states.

On a clear day, the magnificent peak of the mountain can be seen over one hundred miles away. It is encircled by a stupendous forest, with Douglas fir, red cedars and western hemlock, some of them soaring more than 200 feet above mossy, fern–draped valley floors.

When one is in the park, it is easy to understand the words of a Stanford University professor: 'I have seen the glories of Switzerland, the grandeur of the Andes and the grace of the beautiful cone of Fujiyama, but among the most renowned scenery of the world, I know of nothing more majestic or more inspiring than the grandeur of my own camping ground, Mount Rainier.' The 14,410–foot peak has this effect on everyone who comes to it.

*Opposite far left*: An autumn view of Reflection Lake with Mount Rainier in the background. The mountain was first scaled by two young men, Philemon Beecher Van Trump and Hazard Stevens, in 1870.

*Left*: Summer wildflowers with Mount Rainier in the background. In the subalpine meadows near the mountain can be found all manner of beautiful blooms during the summer months.

*Following page*: Mount Rainier, looking over the Carbon River. The mountain juts its glacier-furrowed snow-cloaked brow toward the heavens—the majestic symbol of the Northwest's natural grandeur.

*Below*: Some of the gorgeous wildflowers to be found in Mount Rainier National Park— broadleaf lupine (*Lupinus latifolius*) and sitka valerian (*Valerian sitchenensis*) in the Tatoosh Range of the park.

# NORTH CASCADES

North Cascades National Park, established in 1968, covers 504,781 acres (789 square miles) in northcentral Washington State along the border with British Columbia, Canada. This is a spectacular mountain region with many glacier lakes, and containing some of America's most breathtakingly beautiful scenery. There are high jagged peaks, ridges, slopes and countless cascading waterfalls. The park encompasses some 318 glaciers, which is more than half of all the glaciers in the lower 48 states. Rumbling sounds frequently interrupt the subalpine stillness as icefalls crash into the valley floor from glaciers that seem to be ever so precariously perched on the many steep mountain slopes.

Even though early Indians left some imprints on the land, history has touched little of the park complex, and some remote locations have yet to feel the boots of the backcountry traveler. Forest giants of western red cedar and Douglas fir dot the deep valleys. Tangled growths of vine maple, stinging nettles and devil's club still defy cross–country hikers. Glaciers scored by crevasses, permanent snowfields and sheer–walled cliffs, spires and pinnacles challenge the mountaineer. Rainbow trout, Dolly Varden, brook trout and golden trout are found in the many streams and the mountain and valley lakes. As one writer said: 'Nowhere do the mountain masses and peaks present such fantastic, dauntless and startling outlines.'

**Mountains of the North Cascades National Park. Recent historical exploration of the region began in 1814 when Alexander Ross crossed the present national park's south end. A handful of explorers followed him over the years.**

**The explorers commented on the region's rugged, isolated nature. Miners prospected for gold, lead, zinc and platinum from 1880 to 1910. Some logging and homesteading occurred around 1900. Today the Skagit River generates electricity.**

*Right*: Sawtooth Ridge and Fisher Creek in North Cascades National Park, Washington.

*Below*: Giant fern shoots in North Cascade National Park with the mountains in the background. In this area can sometimes be seen mountain goats, deer, black bear, wolverines, martens, fishers, grizzly bear, cougar and moose. White-tailed ptarmigans and bald eagles as well as many other smaller birds can be occasionally spotted.

# OLYMPIC

Olympic National Park encompasses 914,579 acres (1429 square miles) of mountain wilderness, containing the finest remnant of a Pacific Northwest rain forest, as well as active glaciers, a Pacific shoreline and a rare breed of animal—the Olympic elk. Established in 1938 the park dominates Washington State's northwestern Olympic Peninsula.

Olympic is a gift from the sea. Clouds borne on the moist sea winds, rain and snow wrung from the clouds by the heights, and glaciers and rivers returning seaward mold this park's magnificent shoreline, nurture the Pacific Northwest rain forest, mantle rugged peaks in snow and sculpt the slopes from the high peaks to the valleys.

Botanists point out that the temperate rain forest here is one of the few on earth. Here can be seen great stands of western hemlock, Sitka spruce, western red cedar, bigleaf maple and other species of trees. Overhanging branches are draped with air–loving club mosses and lichens. Everything looks green—including the air.

The mountains of the Olympic Range are formidable— and geologically new. Their sharp, forceful peaks are products of both continental drift, or plate tectonics, and volcanism. Only the elements challenge their supremacy, in the process creating a battle between erosion and upthrust that ebbs and flows continually. For the moment the mountains are the master, since their height controls the weather.

*Left*: **Logs in a stream in the Quinault Valley Rain Forest in Olympic National Park, Washington. This area of the park was created by an ancient glacier, which also was resonsible for nearby Lake Quinault.**

*Below*: **A panoramic scene of Olympic National Park, taken from the summit of Mount Ferry.**

*Overleaf*: **The surf and rocks at sunset at Rialto Beach in the Olympic Seashore area of Olympic National Park.**

# PETRIFIED FOREST

Petrified Forest National Park, established in 1962, covers 93,493 acres (146 square miles) near Holbrook, Arizona. It not only contains extensive petrified wood—the remains of trees—and Indian artifacts, but also part of the Painted Desert. The Blue Mesa, Jasper, Crystal and Rainbow forests are where the best and most colorful specimens of petrified trees can be seen. The sides of Newspaper Rock are inscribed with a large number of ancient Indian petroglyphs. There is also the 111–foot–long Agate Bridge—a single petrified tree spanning a 40–foot–deep arroyo, and Agate House, a partially restored Pueblo dwelling built 900 years ago from petrified wood.

Two hundred million years ago the area was a floodplain with nearby tall, stately pine–like trees. They fell and were washed by streams into the floodplain, where they were covered by silt, mud and volcanic ash, which cut off oxygen and slowed decay. Silica–bearing ground waters seeped through the logs, replacing the original wood tissues with silica deposits. The silicas hardened and the logs were preserved as petrified wood. When the area lifted, the logs emerged from under the water.

**Top**: Petrified logs in Jasper Forest in Petrified Forest National Park. Jasper Forest shows the area's typical topography and some of the petrified logs with root systems still attached indicate that they grew nearby.

**Right**: Blue Mesa in the morning. This area's colorful banded buttes, mesas and cones clearly reveal the ancient layers of the floodplain.

# REDWOOD

Redwood National Park near Crescent City, California, was established in 1968 and contains 110,131 acres (172 square miles) along 40 miles of Pacific coastline, filled with groves of ancient redwoods—the world's tallest trees. The tallest redwood known to man soars upwards to 367.8 feet—a greater distance than the length of a football field.

Coast redwoods have been known to live to be 2000 years old, and the average life span is probably from 500 to 700 years. The living tree has no killing diseases, and the insects associated with it cause no significant damage. Since the trees lack taproots, however, many of them are toppled by the wind.

The first record of the redwood was written by Fray Juan Crespi in 1769. Its botanical discoverer was Archibald Menzies, whose collections are dated 1794. The name 'redwood' comes from the Spanish word for the tree, palo colorado, which means 'red tree.'

The park has a vast number of different habitats for animals. It is on the Pacific Flyway, and more than 300 species of birds can be seen here. Offshore, gray whales migrate, as well as porpoises, seals, and sea lions. In the park are Roosevelt elk, mountain lions, blacktail deer, river otters, mink and beaver, plus just one poisonous snake—the Northern Pacific Rattlesnake.

*Below*: **Towering giant redwoods in Redwood National Park. Much of the North American Continent was covered with redwoods until the Ice Age.**

*Opposite*: **An afternoon shot in Redwood National Park. Ferns cover the forest floor and giant trees rise toward the sky. Note the redwood sapling.**

# ROCKY MOUNTAIN

Rocky Mountain National Park in northern Colorado is one of the older national parks, having been established in 1915. Covering 266,944 acres (417 square miles), and straddling the Continental Divide, it contains 107 named peaks that are over 11,000 feet high—the highest being Long Peak at 14,256 feet.

The snow–mantled peaks of the park rise above verdant alpine valleys and glistening lakes. One–third of the park is above the tree line, and here the tundra predominates. The area was first crossed by settlers in 1859 when Joel Estes and his son Milton rode into the valley that bears their name.

At lower levels, open stands of ponderosa pine and juniper grow on the slopes facing the sun; on cooler northern slopes are Douglas fir. Gracing the streamsides are blue spruces intermixed with dense stands of lodgepole pines. Here and there are groves of aspen, and wildflowers dot the meadows and glades. Above 9000 feet forests of Englemann spruce and subalpine fir take over, and the beautiful wildflower, the Colorado columbine, reigns.

*Above*: Rocky Mountain National Park has some stark scenery. Here, trees buffeted by winds and exposed to the elements try to hold their own in the rocky soil.

*Left*: Alberta Falls in Rocky Mountain National Park, Colorado. The area is a wildlife sanctuary, with deer, wapiti (American elk), bighorn sheep, beaver and other animals.

*Opposite left*: A morning shot of Bear Lake in the autumn— Front Range, Rocky Mountain National Park. This alpine lake was the product of glaciation and is surrounded by subalpine life.

*Following page*: Another view of Bear Lake, located in the east central part of Rocky Mountain National Park. In the distance is Hallett Peak, 12,713 feet high, and located in the Front Range.

# SEQUOIA

Sequoia National Park is one of the oldest national parks, having been established in 1890. Located east of Fresno, California and bordering Kings Canyon National Park, it covers 402,488 acres (629 square miles) and contains groves of giant sequoias, the world's oldest trees, and the highest mountain in the lower 48 states, Mount Whitney, with a height of 14,494 feet.

But Mount Whitney does not stand alone, although it caps the Sierra Nevada that John Muir once termed 'The Range of Light.' Many peaks in the park are more than 14,000 feet above sea level. There are also spectacular valleys.

The rocks of the foothills and summits indicate that this whole region once lay under the ocean. The Sierra Nevada itself is a huge block of the earth's crust which, over millions of years, was uplifted by various geological phenomena and then tilted slightly west.

The sequoia tree, for which this park was named, is a unique plant. Some of the sequoias, the kings of the conifers, now standing in the Sierra Nevada, were nodding their lofty boughs in Biblical days. And after 70 more generations of man, they will, most probably, still flourish in cool California summers and mountain winters that bring six feet of snow and zero temperatures.

The sequoias and the redwoods are, since the glacial period, the only American survivors of an ancient species that spread as far north as the Arctic Zone. Sequoias may attain a height of 300 feet, with a diameter of 30 feet above the stump–swell. Many of them are 2000 years old; on one tree stump 3400 growth rings were recorded, and John Muir reported counting 4000 rings on another. They are almost indestructable. Their bark is up to 24 inches thick with a layer of scales that is hard to burn.

**Sunrise on the Mount Whitney group of peaks—February. The photo was taken from the Lower Boy Scout Lake Basin in the John Muir Wilderness section.**

*Above*: Looking upwards at giant sequoias in the morning fog—Giant Forest of Sequoia National Park. A mature tree will produce more than 2000 cones per year with nearly a half million seeds. And the cones may stay on the trees for up to 20 years.

*Right*: 'The Senate,' a group of sequoia trees in Congress Grove, Sequoia National Park. Few records show mature sequoias ever having died of disease or insect attack. They usually die by being toppled by the wind or a bolt of lightning.

# SHENANDOAH

Shenandoah National Park lies in the heart of the Blue Ridge Mountains of Virginia. Authorized in 1926, it covers 195,057 acres (305 square miles) and overlooks the beautiful Shenandoah Valley. Front Royal is the northern gateway to the park, which is 75 miles long and features mountains where scenic highways and trails wind around ridges and valleys, streams, waterfalls and fields of flowers.

With every day–to–day or moment–to–moment change of the weather, the mood of Shenandoah changes. Low–lying clouds, snow, mist, autumn colors and the sun's rays at dawn and dusk, all affect the scenic beauty of the park. Trails totaling more than 500 miles make much of the park accessible to hikers. More than 95 percent of the park is covered by forests with about 100 species of trees. Two–fifths of the park has been designated by the US Congress as wilderness.

Here may be found deer, bear, bobcats, chipmunks, raccoons, skunks, opossums and gray squirrels. The park is filled with birds—turkeys, ruffed grouse, barred owls, ravens, woodpeckers, juncoes, flycatchers, thrushes, vireos, 35 species of warblers, and almost 200 species of other birds.

*Left*: **An autumn afternoon at Dark Hollow Falls in the Blue Ridge Mountains—Shenandoah National Park, Virginia. The waterfall cascades some 70 feet over greenstone.**

*Below*: **Autumn foliage along the Skyline Drive in Shenandoah National Park. Fall is the season of brilliant colors and clear, crisp days, and people come for miles to see the autumn coloration.**

# THEODORE ROOSEVELT

Theodore Roosevelt National Park is located in western North Dakota near Watford City. Established in 1978, it covers 70,416 acres (110 square miles) and includes part of Roosevelt's ranch and the scenic badlands. In the park also are colorful conical hills, buttes and tablelands; a burning lignite coal vein; remnants of petrified forests; varied flora, including yucca and cactus; a prairie dog town, plus birds, deer, antelope, buffalo and smaller animals and a museum at Medora, North Dakota.

When Theodore Roosevelt was a young New York assemblyman, he arrived in the Badlands in September 1883 for a buffalo hunt. Before returning to the East Coast, he joined two other men as a partner in the Maltese Cross Ranch. As a consequence of his observations of the decline of wildlife in the Badlands and in the West, Roosevelt organized the Boone and Crockett Club in 1887, which lobbied for the 1891 Forest Reserve Act and the 1894 Park Protection Act. As president, he fostered the establishment of the US Forest Service and signed the Antiquities Act, which enabled him to proclaim 18 national monuments and obtain Congressional approval for the establishment of five national parks.

*Top*: **Sunset on the North Dakota Badlands in the South Unit of Theodore Roosevelt National Park, which is near Medora and is separated from the North Unit by several miles.**

*Left*: **Sunrise over Painted Canyon in the Badlands of the South Unit of Theodore Roosevelt National Park. Much of the area is composed of blue bentonite clay.**

*Opposite*: **Autumn coloration on the Shenandoah Ridges, from Hazel Mountain Overlook, Shenandoah.**

# VIRGIN ISLANDS

Virgin Islands National Park encompasses 14,695 acres (23 square miles) on St John Island in the Virgin Islands, and that area makes up about 75 percent of the whole island. Authorized in 1956, the park contains lush vegetation, lovely white sand beaches, Indian relics and some evidence that it was once occupied by colonial Danes.

Growing from the rocky outcrops bordering numerous bays and from small rocky cays, or islands, are the coral reefs. These fringing reefs are a complex community of interesting and interacting plants and animals.

The basic building blocks of reefs are hard corals—including brain, elkhorn, star, finger and staghorn—and soft corals—especially sea fans and sea whips. With the corals are a variety of fishes, including parrot fish, surgeon, angelfish, grunts, butterfly-fish, blueheads, wrasse and snappers.

Closely dependent on the reefs are the sand beaches for which the park is so well known. Without the growth of the living coral, the beaches could not exist, for the sand here is composed of minute fragments of coral. The reefs also protect the beaches from being washed away by winter ground seas.

**A view of Trunk Bay in Virgin Islands National Park. It has one of the best beaches in the world and offers an underwater nature trail for snorklers.**

# VOYAGEURS

V oyageurs National Park is located on the northern border of Minnesota, near International Falls. Authorized in 1971, this 219,128 acre (342 square mile) park contains abundant lakes, forests and wildlife. Water dominates the Voyageurs landscape. Within its boundaries more than 30 lakes—some huge, some small—fill glacier-carved rock basins. Between these lakes and adjacent rocky knobs and ridges, extend bogs, marshes and beaver ponds.

Named for the *voyageurs* from Canada who traveled through the region in the heyday of the fur trade in the late eighteenth and early nineteenth centuries, the park is the home of a wide variety of animal life. Osprey, eagle and great blue heron nests are found here. Other birds that may be sighted are kingfishers, mergansers, loons and cormorants. Beaver, deer, moose and wolves are also residents. The wolves usually live in packs of two to twelve and during their hunt for food may well cover as much as 40 miles in a single night, running at 30 to 35 miles per hour.

*Left*: **Voyageurs National Park offers many enticements to the sportsman—sailing, boating, camping, swimming, hiking, skiing.**

*Below*: **Most of the park is water, and this probably made it very inviting to the French–Canandian *voyageurs* in their canoes.**

# WRANGELL-ST.ELIAS

Wrangell–St Elias National Park is one of the newer national parks, having been established in 1980, and it is the largest one, covering 8,945,000 acres (13,977 square miles). Located a day's drive east of Anchorage, Alaska, it has abundant wildlife and many mountain peaks, some of them over 16,000 feet high. One of them is Mount St Elias, which, at 18,008 feet, is the second highest mountain in North America, just behind Mount McKinley. The mountains, the glaciers and the snowfields dominate the landscape.

There are more than 100 glaciers in the park and one of them, Malespina, is larger than the state of Rhode Island. The park is a sportman's paradise. Hiking and backpacking trails wind through the valleys and passes; some of the mountains are among the most challenging in the country for mountain climbing; rafting can be exciting on the Bremner, Chitina and Copper Rivers. Wrangell–St Elias borders on the Kluane National Park in Canada's Yukon Territory, and together they have been placed on the United Nations list of outstanding natural areas.

**Mount Sanford in Wrangell–St Elias National Park is a mountain climber's dream.**

# YELLOWSTONE

Yellowstone National Park, the nation's first national park, established in 1872, is located in Northwestern Wyoming, Idaho and Montana. The park, covering 2,219,823 acres (3468 square miles) contains the world's largest geyser area—some 3000 geysers and hot springs—spectacular waterfalls and impressive canyons.

Elk, moose, deer, bison, antelope, coyote and bear are abundant in the park. But probably the park's favorite attraction is the dependable Old Faithful Geyser. Its eruption times are so predictable that the time of the next eruption is posted at the Old Faithful Visitor Center.

The Grand Canyon of the Yellowstone leaves many people breathless. Here one can look down at the deceptively tiny river, at wisps of steam, at the pastel canyon walls. Ospreys wheel and soar above the canyon bottom. At the Lower Falls, the bottle–green Yellowstone River breaks into frothy white jets as it drops away 309 feet into the canyon below.

Yellowstone Lake is a mixture of charm on placid summer days, anger during sudden storms and beauty in the quiet of a glorious evening sunset reflected on the Absaroka Mountains.

*Left*: **The Lower Falls of the Grand Canyon of the Yellowstone, taken in the afternoon from Artist Point.**
*Below*: **Fog at sunrise over Gibbon Meadow in Yellowstone National Park in October.**

*Right*: An eruption of Old Faithful Geyser. Old Faithful erupts on an average of every 71 minutes, although this can vary from 33 to 148 minutes. Still, it is the star of Yellowstone National Park, since it hasn't missed a performance in the more than 100 years since its discovery.

*Below*: The Riverside Geyser erupts—Upper Geyser Basin, Yellowstone National Park. Riverside shares the Upper Geyser Basin with Old Faithful, and the Grand, Castle and Beehive Geysers, among others. One of the most predictable in the park, Riverside erupts every five and three quarter hours.

*Bottom*: Firehole Falls in the morning. The Firehole River, on which the falls are located, passes through the Upper Geyser Basin quite near the geysers located there.

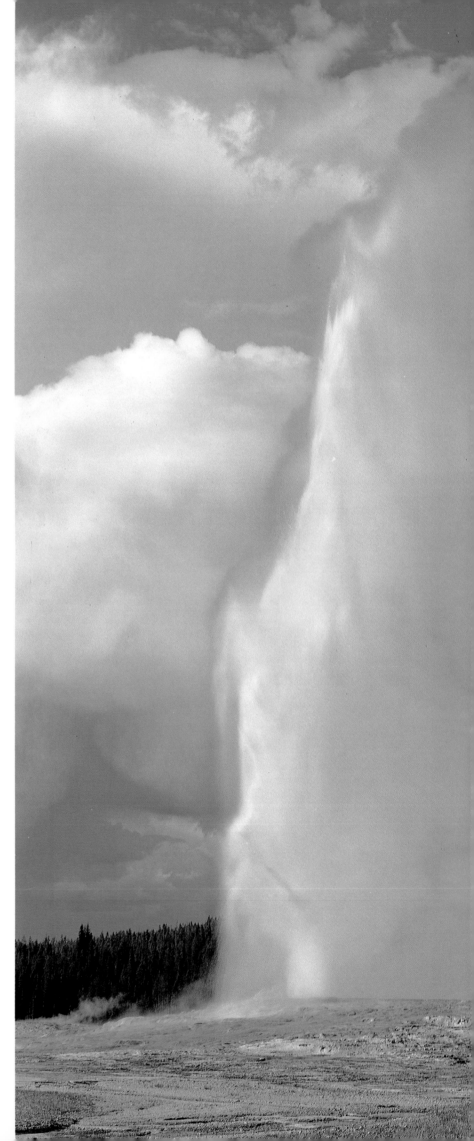

*Above*: An eruption of the Great Fountain Geyser in Yellowstone National Park.

*Overleaf:* Yellowstone Falls. The Upper Falls of the Yellowstone are 109 feet high and the Lower Falls are 308 feet high. The water plunges over these falls and then flows through Yellowstone Canyon. The Yellowstone River flows 671 miles from the continental Divide in northwestern Wyoming to the Missouri River on the Montana–North Dakota line.

# YOSEMITE

Yosemite National Park is an old park—established in 1890—and covers an area of 760,917 acres (1189 square miles) northeast of Fresno, California. It is a mountainous park and has in it the nation's highest waterfall, plus three groves of sequoia trees.

The park embraces a vast tract of scenic wildlands set aside to preserve a portion of the Sierra Nevada that stretches along California's eastern flank. The park ranges from 2000 feet above sea level to more than 13,000 feet, and offers three major features: alpine wilderness, groves of giant sequoias and Yosemite Valley.

The story of Yosemite began about 500 million years ago when the Sierra Nevada region lay beneath an ancient sea. Thick layers of sediment lay on the sea bed, which eventually was folded and twisted and thrust above sea level. Simultaneously, molten rock welled up from deep within the earth and cooled slowly beneath the layers of sediment to form granite. Erosion gradually wore away almost all the overlying rock and exposed the granite. Even as uplifts continued, water and then glaciers carved the face of Yosemite.

**Right**: Yosemite Falls, taken from Leidig Meadow of Yosemite National Park. This is the highest waterfall in the United States—1750 feet high—about ten times the height of Niagara.
**Opposite**: Half Dome at sunset, looking from Yosemite Valley. This rock mass rises to a height of 8852 feet at the head of the valley. At its base is beautiful Mirror Lake.
**Below**: Morning at Three Brothers in the Yosemite Valley.

Nevada Falls pours over giant steps formed by
the action of glaciers. Liberty Cap is in the background.

The Merced River with Half Dome in the background.
This seemingly-peaceful river carved Merced Canyon.

**Tuolumne River Canyon in Yosemite National Park. The elevation here is about 8500 feet.**

# ZION

Zion National Park, 'The Rainbow of the Desert,' is located in southwestern Utah. Established in 1919 it covers 146,551 acres (229 square miles) of unusual rock formations and landscapes. It embraces one of the West's most grandiose gorges—multicolored, rock–temple–filled Zion Canyon—formed in part by the Virgin River.

Zion Canyon, one of the most beautifully colored canyons in the world, is about 15 miles long and from half a mile to only a few feet wide. Its walls tower 2000 to 3000 feet, and in some places are almost straight up and down. The canyon contains many unusual rock formations, including the Great White Throne, a huge mass of stone rising nearly half a mile from the canyon floor. The colorful throne may reflect purple at one moment and pale yellow the next.

There are other colorful canyons in the park, some of which are extremely narrow and have steep, plunging walls. Rock formations range in color from dark red and orange to light purple and pink. These colors change continuously with the reflection of the light.

Wild animal and plant life flourish in the park. Mule deer and smaller animals live in the canyons, and a few bighorn, or mountain sheep dwell on the many high cliffs of the park.

*Left*: A spectacular waterfall in Zion National Park. The trees in the foreground are cottonwoods and are located in The Temple of Sinawava, a natural amphitheater.

*Opposite top*: The Virgin River in Zion Canyon. This placid stream may become a raging torrent during spring runoffs and after a sudden summer storm, depositing debris at every turn—logs, rocks and other materials from many miles distant. Thus it is an important erosion force.

*Opposite bottom*: Autumn near the Three Patriarchs in Zion Canyon.

*Below*: The West Temple, Towers of the Virgin in winter.

*Overleaf*: Cottonwoods framing The Sentinel in Zion National Park.